GROW IN HIS WORD
New Testament
Part 3: The Christ

A 13-Lesson Survey Study
of the Life of Jesus Christ

Part THREE of a four-part study of the entire Bible

By Dennis R. Miller

Part of the GROW Ministries
Fort Wayne, Indiana 46814

Contact us at: growministries@me.com

*(Information on Leader's Guides and other teaching and learning
resources can be found on the next page.)*

© Copyright 1987

Revised 1995, 2005, 2006, 2007, 2008, 2009, 2011, 2014, 2020

A Short History of This Course

I hadn't been in the pastoral ministry very long when I realized that many Christians are unable to use their Bibles effectively. In fact, many people are even unable to find their way around the Book of Books. For me, one of the first steps in really understanding a book or topic is to first understand the "big picture" or survey.

As I began teaching this survey I realized that most Christians had never really seen the "big picture" of the Word. And as they began to see it, suddenly much of their previous learning began to make much more sense to them. It has been fun to watch the expressions of understanding as the Bible began to unfold in a new way.

I have now been teaching this Bible survey for more than 35 years. It is a compilation of the things that I have learned and taught and I'm sure that it will continue to grow and develop. My hope is that you will grasp this survey and that it will enhance your knowledge and future study of God's Word.

Dennis R. Miller

Our Theme Verses for This Study

*Psalm 1:1 Blessed is the man
who does not walk in the counsel of the wicked
or stand in the way of sinners
or sit in the seat of mockers.
2 But his delight is in the law of the LORD,
and on his law he meditates day and night.
3 He is like a tree planted by streams of water,
which yields its fruit in season
and whose leaf does not wither.
Whatever he does prospers.*

FOR TEACHERS OR INDIVIDUAL STUDIES:

The **Leader's Guide** for this book can be purchased on Amazon in paperback or Kindle formats.

The **Keynote** or **Powerpoint** files, **audio files** and **video teaching** (for teachers or for someone wishing to do this study personally) are available at http://growministriesonline.com.

Photos, organized by geographical locations, and other teaching resources are available for use by GROW teachers and can be found here: https://www.flickr.com/photos/growministries/albums

A Survey of the Bible

You are in the process of a 52-lesson study of the entire Bible which is broken down into four 13-lesson sections. This course will take you all the way through the Bible and, although you will not read every chapter, you will be reading much of the Bible throughout your study.

A survey is something like looking through a newspaper and only reading the headlines. Although you will be reading more than headlines during this study, doing in-depth, verse-by-verse study will come later.

Many Christians do not have a good grasp of the message and flow of the Bible. The purpose of this course is to give you confidence with your Bible.

Although this book is designed for the learning of content and flow it is also important that we apply the lessons that we learn, so application questions are included with each lesson. It is also important to build quality relationships with other Christians. This will provide accountability as those relationships continue to build.

Study hard, ask lots of questions and interact with the other students and you will find this course helpful in learning the "headlines" of God's Word.

What You Will Need

1. **Your Bible** – A study Bible is best. If you do not have one this would be a good time to purchase it. Make sure to use the translation that the rest of the group will use and use the same translation for the entire course. Mark it up and make it yours!

2. **Time** – You will need to set aside time each week to do the reading and write down a few reactions. This course is almost useless if you do not do the readings.

3. **This workbook** – Make sure to bring this workbook to every class. There is plenty of room for notes. Your leader will follow this guide so you will want to have it with you. When you are finished, the workbook will be a resource book for you.

If you are doing a self-study, you can find audio files of the teaching and other aids here: *http://growministriesonline.com*

For Additional Insights:

You can purchase the book, <u>What the Bible Is All About</u> by Henrietta Mears. This book was written in the 1950's but is still one of the best overviews of Scripture available. If you read this along with your Bible each week, you will gain many extra insights. This book is available on Amazon.

Overview

Overview of the 52-Lesson Study of Old and New Testaments

	Part 1 Old Testament The People	Part 2 Old Testament The Prophets	Part 3 New Testament The Christ	Part 4 New Testament The Church
1	STAGES	Poetry and Prophecy - Introduction and Review	Introduction - Review and REPORT	REPORT and Early Church
2	Starting	Job	The Gospels	Early Church
3	Starting	Psalms	Redeemer - INCARNATE	Paul's Ministry
4	Treaties and Tribes	Proverbs	Redeemer - Incarnation	Paul's Ministry
5	Treaties and Tribes	Ecclesiastes	Redeemer - NoWhere	Paul's Ministry - Letters on Conduct
6	Advancement	Song of Songs	Redeemer - Confirmed	Paul's Ministry - Letters on Creed
7	Advancement	Isaiah	Redeemer - Admired	Paul's Ministry - Letters on Christ
8	Advancement	Jeremiah & Lamentations	Redeemer - Rejected	Paul's Ministry - Letters on Church
9	Glory	Ezekiel	Redeemer - NowHere	Paul's Ministry - Letters on Coming
10	Glory	Daniel	Redeemer - Abhorred/Adored	One Church - Letters to Hebrew Christians
11	Erosion	Daniel	Redeemer - The Passion	One Church - Letters by the Apostles
12	Servitude	Minor Prophets	Redeemer - The Passion	One Church - The Revelation
13	Servitude	Malachi and Between the Testaments	Redeemer - Exalted	One Church, Reformation, Revival & Today
	The Story of the Chosen People and Their History Which Leads to the Christ	**The Study of the Poets and Prophets Who Spoke of the Coming Messiah**	**The Story of the Messiah's Life and the Fulfillment of Prophecy**	**The Story of the Christian Church from Acts, the Letters and Beyond**

Reading Schedule
Suggested Reading and Memorization by Lesson

Date	#	New Testament The Church	Reading Assignment	Learn/Memorize	Mears Book Chapters
	1	Introduction - Review and REPORT			
	2	The Gospels	Matthew 21:1-11; Mark 11:1-11; Luke 19:28-44; John 12:12-19	Focus of each gospel and audience	26
	3	Redeemer - INCARNATE	John 1	INCARNATE	27
	4	Redeemer - Incarnation	Luke 1-2	INCARNATE	27
	5	Redeemer - NoWhere	Luke 2:41-52; Matthew 2	Books of the New Testament	28
	6	Redeemer - Confirmed	Luke 3:1 - 4:13; John 2:1-11	Books of the New Testament	28
	7	Redeemer - Admired	Luke 4-8; Matthew 5-7	Sub words of the I-N-C of INCARNATE	29
	8	Redeemer - Rejected	Luke 9:51-62; Matthew 11-12; John 7-10	Twelve Apostles	29
	9	Redeemer - NowHere	Matthew 16; Luke 9-12	Twelve Apostles	30
	10	Redeemer - Abhorred/Adored	Luke 13:1 - 19:27	Sub words of the A-R-N of INCARNATE	30
	11	Redeemer - The Passion	Luke 19:1 - 22:71	Philippians 2:6-11	
	12	Redeemer - The Passion	Luke 23	Philippians 2:6-11	
	13	Redeemer - Exalted	Luke 24	Sub words of INCARNATE	38

The Hall of Fame Chapters

You do not need to memorize the chapter numbers and titles below, but you should be very familiar with them. These chapters are ones that people who know the Bible well are normally able to identify when someone refers to them. You won't be sorry if you take time to learn them.

The Gospels

1. Matthew 1 and Luke 3   The Genealogies of Christ

2. Matthew 5   The Beatitudes

3. Matthew 6:9-13   The Lord's Prayer

4. Matthew 5-7   The Sermon on the Mount

5. Matthew 10   The Discipleship Chapter

6. Matthew 16   Peter's Confession of Christ

7. Matthew 23   The Seven Woes

8. Matthew 24-25   The Signs of the End of the Age

9. Matthew 28:18-20   The Great Commission

10. Luke 2   Traditional Christmas Story

11. Luke 15   The Lost Sheep, Coin and Son

12. Luke 24   The Resurrection

13. John 1   The Word

14. John 10   The Shepherd and His Flock

15. John 13   The Washing of the Disciples' Feet

16. John 15   The Vine and the Branches

17. John 17   The Priestly Prayer of Jesus

The New Testament

History	**Letters**	**Prophecy**
5	**21**	**1**
Matthew	Romans	The Revelation
Mark	1 & 2 Corinthians	
Luke	Galatians	
John	Ephesians	
Acts	Philippians	
	Colossians	
	1 & 2 Thessalonians	
	1 & 2 Timothy	
	Titus	
	Philemon	
	Hebrews	
	James	
	1 & 2 Peter	
	1, 2 & 3 John	
	Jude	

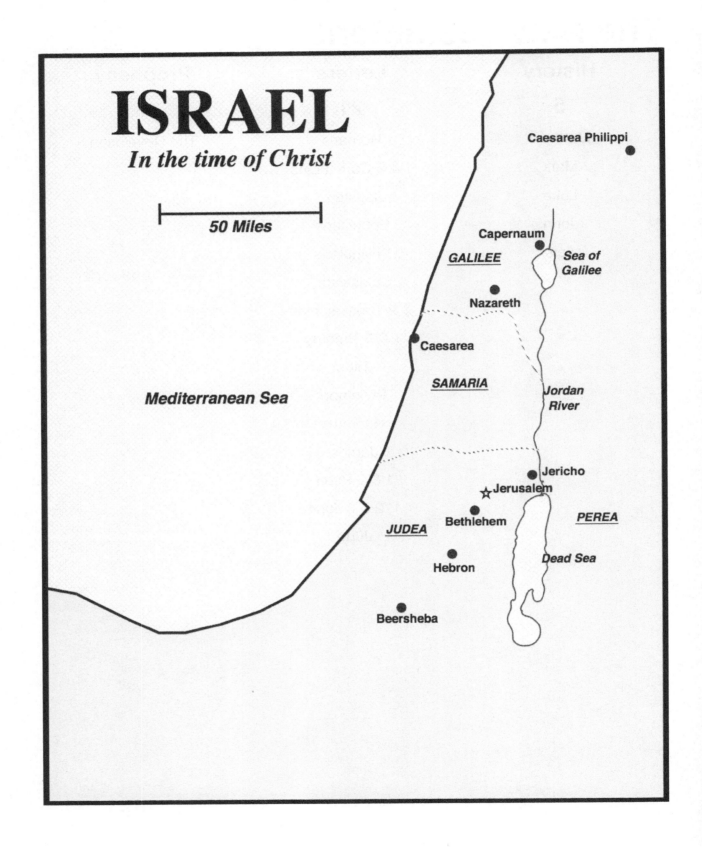

Introduction
Review and REPORT

Lesson 1

As we get started in our study of the Scriptures we will learn why the New Testament was written and also quickly review what we have learned about the Old Testament.

The Importance of Knowing the Bible

Mark 12:24 Jesus replied, "Are you not in error because you do not know the Scriptures or the power of God?

2 Tim. 2:15 Do your best to present yourself to God as one approved, a workman who does not need to be ashamed and who correctly handles the word of truth.

A Review

The Bible contains __56__ books written by more than __40__ authors over a period of __1500__ years! And yet, it has one central theme and focus: the __glory of God__ _____ through the __Redemption__ of man.

The true Author of the Scriptures is, of course, the __Holy Spirit__.

2 Pet. 1:21 For prophecy never had its origin in the will of man, but men spoke from God as they were carried along by the Holy Spirit.

The Old Testament is the story of Jesus Christ __foretold__.
The New Testament is the story of Jesus Christ __fulfilled__.

Introduction

What Is the Purpose of the New Testament?

1. to complete the *Revelation* of the Old Testament

   Heb. 1:1 In the past God spoke to our forefathers through the prophets at many times and in various ways,

2. to show the fulfillment of Old Testament *Prophecy*

   Luke 4:21 and he began by saying to them, "Today this scripture is fulfilled in your hearing."

   John 13:18 "I am not referring to all of you; I know those I have chosen. But this is to fulfill the scripture: 'He who shares my bread has lifted up his heel against me.'

3. to present the *fullness* of the way of *Salvation*

   John 20:31 But these are written that you may believe that Jesus is the Christ, the Son of God, and that by believing you may have life in his name.

4. to _____ and _____ the church

   Matt. 16:18 And I tell you that you are Peter, and on this rock I will build my church, and the gates of Hades will not overcome it.

The REPORT of the New Testament

Luke 7:22 So he replied to the messengers, "Go back and report to John what you have seen and heard: The blind receive sight, the lame walk, those who have leprosy are cured, the deaf hear, the dead are raised, and the good news is preached to the poor.

Period	Events/Men	Date	Where Found?	People to Know
R				
E				
P				
O				
R				
T				

Application

The REPORT acrostic will be an important tool for the coming weeks to help you remember the time line of the New Testament and historical events. Discuss the following question as a class:

• What is your personal plan to memorize the REPORT acrostic and its key events? Write your plan below and then share it with the class or a partner. Some ideas include: copy the notes you took today on to note cards and study them for a few moments each day throughout the week. Or record yourself saying the events and men under each letter of REPORT and then listen to it on your way to and from work or while running errands. Or think of a better idea that would work for you!

thē-ŏl'ə-jē

Redemption — The purchase back of something that had been lost, by the payment of a ransom.

Bryant, T.A. Today's Dictionary of the Bible. Minneapolis, MN: Bethany House Publishers: 1982.

The Gospels

Lesson 2

The first four books of the New Testament are called gospels because they are the "good news" about Jesus Christ. Each of these books is written about the same themes: the birth, life, death and resurrection of Jesus. However, they are written by different men to different audiences which gives each gospel a special flavor. In this lesson we will learn about the four gospels and what they teach.

To prepare for class: Read Matthew 21:1-11; Mark 11:1-11; Luke 19:28-44; John 12:12-19

Write your thoughts and reflections from the reading:

The Gospels

What is a gospel?

Key Thought

Each gospel was written to a specific _____ about a specific _____ for a specific _____ , and yet each gospel is a complete and powerful story of Jesus Christ.

Why Four Gospels?

God's use of numbers —

What does the number four signify?

The Arrangement of the Gospels

The first three gospels are similar and are called _____.

    Why?

The fourth gospel, John, is 90% unique material.

Events of the Four Gospels

Event	Matthew	Mark	Luke	John
Pre-incarnate Christ				1:1-3
Jesus's Birth/ Childhood	1-2		1-2	
John the Baptist	3:1-12	1:1-8	3:1-20	1:6-42
Jesus' Baptism	3:13-17	1:9-11	3:21-22	
The Temptation	4:1-11	1:12-13	4:1-13	
First Miracle				2:1-11
Early Judean Ministry				2:13-4:3
Visit to Samaria				4:4-42
Galilean Ministry	4:12-19:1	1:14-10:1	4:14-9:51	4:43-7:1
Visit to Jerusalem				5:1-47
Perean and Second Galilean Ministry	19-20	10	9:51-19:28	7:2-11
The Last Week	21-27	11-15	19:29-24:1	12-19
Post-resurrection	28	16	24	20-21

Why Are the Gospels Different?

1. They are written to different _____.

2. Each author wrote from his own _____.

3. Each gospel has a different _____.

4. Each author remembered different _____.

5. God _____ it that way!

Gospel Similarities

Each deals with — Christ's...

Christ's...

Christ's...

All of them omit...

Each gospel is complete in itself; however, used together, we have a complete portrait of Jesus Christ.

A Comparison of the Four Gospels

	Matthew	Mark	Luke	John
About the Author				
The Audience				
Key Verse				
Key Word				
Unique Quality				
Arrangement of Material				
Shows Christ as…				
Things to Remember				
Book Referred to as…				
Other				

An Overview of the Four Gospels

Matthew wrote to the _____ about a _____.

Mark wrote to the _____ about a _____ .

Luke wrote to the _____ about a _____ _____.

John wrote to the _____ about a _____ .

The Four Types of Men — Then and Today

A Jew —

A Roman —

A Greek —

All men —

Application

We study the four gospels in this lesson and compare and contrast their differences and similarities. Discuss the following thoughts and questions with your class based on what you just learned:

- In this lesson we learn that each gospel writer had a unique personality and giftedness and therefore wrote about the aspects of Christ's character and ministry that meant the most to him personally as well as his audience. To illustrate that each one of us is drawn to share different characteristics of Christ and His ministry, go around the room and have each person share one sentence about who Christ is. Did everyone say the same words? Did each person focus on the same characteristic of Christ or time in His ministry?

Redeemer
INCARNATE: The Life of Jesus Christ

Lesson 3

In this lesson we look at the life of Jesus Christ from His birth to the ascension, and we will learn a word, INCARNATE, to remember the order of the events of His life. We will then study this word, and the various events of His life, throughout the remainder of this study.

To prepare for class: Read John 1

Write your thoughts and reflections from the reading:

The Life of Jesus Christ
Where Was Jesus Before He Came to Bethlehem?

Jesus was not _____.

He is the _____ member of the Godhead.

What Does John Tell Us About Jesus Before He Came To Earth?

1. Jesus was there…

2. He was involved in the…

3. Jesus is the _____ ___ _____.

4. Jesus was made _____.

5. Jesus was not _____ by His _____ people.

What Do We Learn From Philippians 2?

1. Jesus was, by nature, _____.

2. He gave up His _____ by _____.

3. He knew that He would _____.

4. He shall someday be _____.

It is important that you learn the cities and bodies of water in the map below.

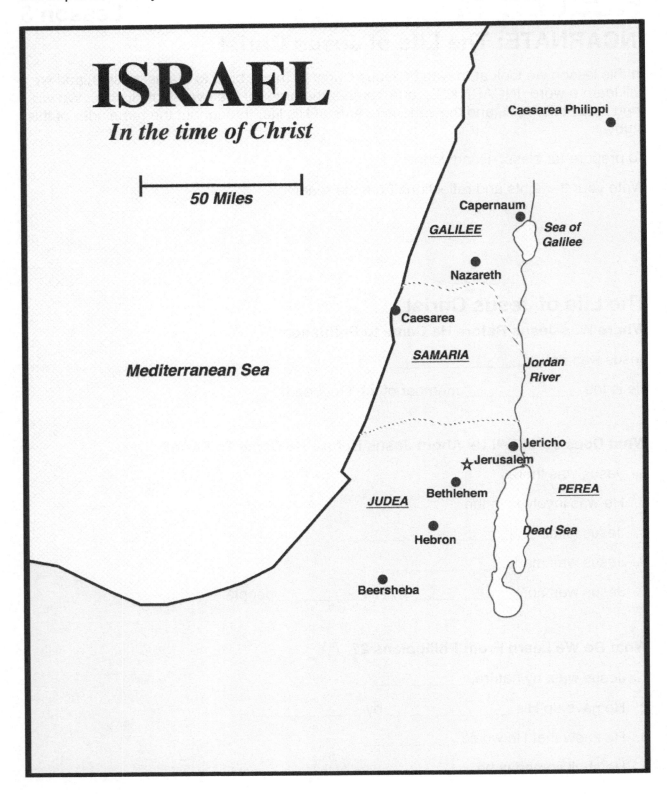

INCARNATE: The Life of Christ

Period	Events	Matthew	Mark	Luke	John	Length
Pre-Incarnate			1:1-6		1	
I		1		1 - 2:1-7, 2:8-20, 2:21-40		8 days
N		2		2:41-51		30 years
C		3, 4	1	3, 4	3, 2	1 year
A		5-7, 8-9, 10:1-4	3:13-19	4-5, 6-8		1 year
R				4:16-30, 9:51-56	6:60-71	1 year (but through-out)
N		16, 17	9	9:18-22, 9:28-34, 10		3-6 months
A				11-18	11, 12	3-6 months
T		21:1-11, 21:12-13	22	19:28-44, 19:45-47, 20-21, 23		5-7 days
E				24		40 days

Application

This lesson is a general overview of the INCARNATE acrostic and map. Discuss these follow-up questions as a group:

- Of all the letters in the INCARNATE acrostic, with which time period in Christ's life are you already most familiar? With which time period of Christ's life are you least familiar? This week read the Scripture passages listed in the Scripture column beside the INCARNATE letter about which you know the least. If time allows, read it right now!

Redeemer
Lesson 4

Incarnation

In this lesson we will learn the first stage of the life of Christ—Incarnation. Over the next nine weeks we will learn eight more stages of Christ's life. These first stages deal with the birth of Christ and the first years of His life.

To prepare for class: Read Luke 1-2

Write your thoughts and reflections from the reading:

The Period of Incarnation

We will study three events during this period:

1. *Virgin birth*
2. *Visit by shepherd*
3. *veneration at temple &*

Greek vs Hebrew

In this period Jesus becomes flesh.

Virgin Birth

(Luke 1:26-38)

The prophecy of Isaiah — *sign*

The words to Joseph from the angel *Luke*

The words to Mary from Gabriel — *Mathew*

The words of Mary —

Mary, the Mother of Jesus

Her name means ___Bitter___.

She was a woman of ___Godliness___.

She is not to be ___Worshipped___.

Luke 11:27 As Jesus was saying these things, a woman in the crowd called out, "Blessed is the mother who gave you birth and nursed you." 28 He replied, "Blessed rather are those who hear the word of God and obey it."

The Genealogies of Christ

In Matthew 1 —

   lineage of ___Joseph___

   _____ line

   _____ order

   There are five great ___Kings___.

14 gen abra
14 " David David child
14- child

   There are four ___Women___.
   Tamar   Ruth
   Rahah   Bathsheba
   There are three ___Eras___.

   There are two ___Fathers___.
   David
   Abraham

In Luke 3 —

   lineage of ___Mary___

   ___Blood___ line

   ___Descending___ order

It goes back to ___Adam___.

It contains no ___Women___ or

   ___ ___time___.

The Genealogies of Christ

Jesus of Nazareth

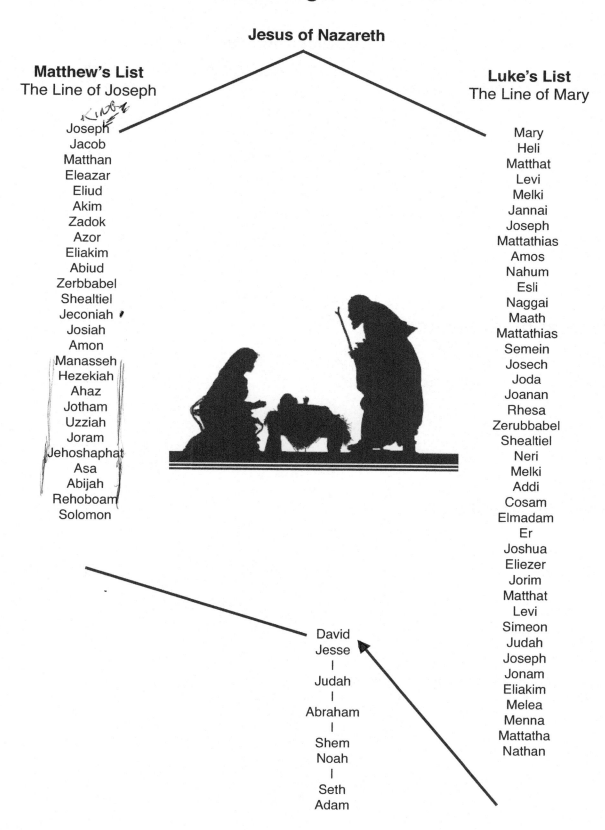

Matthew's List
The Line of Joseph

KING

Joseph
Jacob
Matthan
Eleazar
Eliud
Akim
Zadok
Azor
Eliakim
Abiud
Zerbbabel
Shealtiel
Jeconiah
Josiah
Amon
Manasseh
Hezekiah
Ahaz
Jotham
Uzziah
Joram
Jehoshaphat
Asa
Abijah
Rehoboam
Solomon

Luke's List
The Line of Mary

Mary
Heli
Matthat
Levi
Melki
Jannai
Joseph
Mattathias
Amos
Nahum
Esli
Naggai
Maath
Mattathias
Semein
Josech
Joda
Joanan
Rhesa
Zerubbabel
Shealtiel
Neri
Melki
Addi
Cosam
Elmadam
Er
Joshua
Eliezer
Jorim
Matthat
Levi
Simeon
Judah
Joseph
Jonam
Eliakim
Melea
Menna
Mattatha
Nathan

David
Jesse
|
Judah
|
Abraham
|
Shem
Noah
|
Seth
Adam

Visited by Shepherds
(Luke 2)

Luke 2:18 and all who heard it were amazed at what the shepherds said to them.

Luke 2:20 The shepherds returned, glorifying and praising God for all the things they had heard and seen, which were just as they had been told.

Common

Veneration at the Temple
(Luke 2:21-40)

Simeon — His life and words

Day 40
Righteous
Devout

Faith spirit
Holy spirit
Waiting for

Anna — Her life and words

fasted
prayed
never left

What is the importance of this story?

Application

This lesson deals with the preexistence and incarnation of Jesus Christ. Take a moment to discuss these thoughts and questions based on what you have just studied about Jesus:

- Philippians 2 is a beautiful passage that teaches us about the humility and obedience of Jesus Christ as He "made Himself nothing" by coming to earth to redeem man. How would you define humility in your own words? Based on your own definition, would you consider yourself humble? If you feel comfortable, share with a partner how you can improve in the area of humility.

---

thē-ŏl′ə-jē

Incarnation — That act of grace whereby Christ took our human nature into union with his divine person—became man.

Bryant, T.A. Today's Dictionary of the Bible. Minneapolis, MN: Bethany House Publishers: 1982.

Redeemer   Lesson 5

NoWhere

In this period which lasts 30 years, the theme seems to be "Where is He?"

To prepare for class: Read Luke 2:41-52; Matthew 2

Write your thoughts and reflections from the reading:

Jesus Christ is NoWhere

We will study three events during this period:

1.

2.

3.

Where Is He? – Magi
(Matthew 2:1-12)

Who were they?

Why were they important to this story?

The star —

The gifts —

    Gold —

    Frankincense —

    Myrrh —

Flight to Egypt —

Where Is He? – Mary
(Luke 2:41-52)

Why did Jesus go to the temple?

Why were people amazed?

The importance of the word "Father" —

Where Is He? - Me
(18 years of silence)

Application

This lesson deals with a period of time in Christ's life where we do not know many details. The Bible only highlights a few events that happened in Christ's childhood. Discuss the following thoughts and questions about this period of Christ's life with your class:

• If you are a parent, have you ever briefly "lost" your child in a store or public place? How did it make you feel? Have one or two people in your class share their stories.

• We learned that when Jesus was a young boy he was left behind in Jerusalem when His family thought he was traveling with them elsewhere in the group. When Mary and Joseph later find Jesus, Mary is in a state of near panic and frustration (as well as relief!). She does not yet understand the "big picture" of Jesus' life and therefore she had not known to look at the Temple for her son. However, later in the passage we read that Mary "treasures up all these things in her heart." Mary does not fully understand, yet she treasures these things in her heart. In the same way, we do not understand the "big picture" of how God will work in our own lives; yet we too should treasure what we learn from God and His Word—even when we do not understand it. Take a moment to share with the class something the Lord is teaching you currently, even if you don't understand it fully.

Redeemer

Lesson 6

Confirmed

This period of the life of Christ is called "Confirmed." This period covers a span of about one year. It is during this period that Jesus begins His ministry.

To prepare for class: Read Luke 3:1 - 4:13; John 2:1-11

Write your thoughts and reflections from the reading:

Jesus Christ is Confirmed

We will study three events during this period:

1.

2.

3.

Water

(Matthew 3:13-17)

John the Baptist —

Who confirms Jesus as the Son of God?

The purpose of Jesus' baptism —

Wilderness
(Matthew 4:1-11)

The purpose of the temptation —

Could Jesus have sinned?

Jesus faced three temptations:

    1.

    2.

    3.

Jesus' method for defeating temptation —

Ps. 119:11 I have hidden your word in my heart that I might not sin against you.

Wine
(John 2:1-11)

Who initiates this miracle?

The importance of this kind of miracle —

The results of this miracle —

Application

This lesson deals with three major events that occurred as Christ's ministry on earth began: His baptism, the temptation and His first miracle. Discuss the following thoughts and questions with your class based on what you have just learned:

- We learned in this lesson that one of the reasons that Jesus is baptized is to set an example for us. Baptism is a public declaration of our acceptance of and commitment to Jesus Christ. Have you been baptized? If so, share you experience briefly with your class. If not, pray and consider the reasons why you have not yet been baptized and you may want to decide right now to sign up for the next baptism service available to you.

- The three temptations of Christ remind us that Christ dealt with physical temptation, the temptation of pride and also the temptation to bypass his suffering for pleasure and ease. We can all relate to these areas of temptation in our own lives. Which area is most difficult for you? Jesus quoted Scripture to Satan to combat temptation. Memorize one verse of Scripture this week that will help you deal with the temptation with which you are currently struggling.

Redeemer
Lesson 7

Admired

During this year Jesus was extremely popular! This is the Jesus that the Jews wanted as a Messiah!

To prepare for class: Read Luke 4-8; Matthew 5-7

Write your thoughts and reflections from the reading:

Jesus Christ is Admired

We will study three events during this period:

1.

2.

3.

Authoritative Teaching
(Matthew 5-7)

Much of the teaching style of Jesus can be found in Matthew 5-7 and in the parables of Jesus from this period.

The Sermon on the Mount (Matthew 5:3-11)

The Beatitudes (Matthew 5:3-11) —

Happy are you when the world is not happy with you.		
#4 - Starved for righteousness will be *filled.*	→	
#3 - Meek will *inherit the earth.*	→	
#2 - Mourners for sin will *be comforted.*	→	
#1 - Pour in Spirit receive *the kingdom of heaven.*	→	

Man to God
God does for us
natural

Man to Man
we do
supernatural

The Lord's Prayer (Matthew 6:9-13) —

This prayer is given as a _____ and is not for _____!

Our Father in heaven, — _____

Hallowed be your name, — _____

Your kingdom come, — _____

Your will be done, on earth as it is in heaven. — _____

Give us today day our daily bread. — _____

And forgive us our debts, as we have forgiven our debtors. — _____

And lead us not into temptation, but deliver us from the evil one. — _____ _____

_____

Parables During This Period

Wedding banquet —

Wise manager —

Fig tree —

Sower —

Wheat and weeds —

Matthew 13 contains _____ parables that Jesus taught during this year.

Of the _____ parables in Matthew, all but _____ begin with "The kingdom of God is like…."

All of Jesus' parables during this period are "_____" parables.

Other themes —

Awesome Power

The catch of fish (Luke 5:1-7) —

The man at the pool healed (John 5:1-8) —

Centurion's servant healed (Matthew 8:5-10) —

The storm calmed (Matthew 8:23-27) —

Paralytic healed (Matthew 9:1-8) —

Jairus' daughter raised to life (Mark 5:21-34) —

Demoniacs healed (Mark 3:1-12) —

Appoints Apostles
(Matthew 10:1-4; Mark 3:13-19; Luke 6:12-16 and Acts 1:13)

How many disciples did Jesus have? _____

What is a disciple? _____

What is an apostle? _____ _____

What Should We Learn About the Apostles?

1. There is importance in the _____ of these lists.

2. There is importance in the _____ of these lists.

3. There is importance in the _____ changes.

4. Four of these men came from _____ families.

5. Five of these men were _____ of _____.

6. Eleven of them were from _____.

7. They were called as _____ and became _____.

Matthew	Mark	Luke
Simon Peter	Simon Peter	Simon Peter
Andrew	James	Andrew
James	John	James
John	Andrew	John
Philip	Philip	Philip
Bartholomew	Bartholomew	Bartholomew
Thomas	Matthew	Matthew
Matthew	Thomas	Thomas
James, Son of Alphaeus	James, Son of Alphaeus	James, Son of Alphaeus
Thaddeus	Thaddeus	Simon the Zealot
Simon the Zealot	Simon the Zealot	Judas, Son of James
Judas Iscariot	Judas Iscariot	Judas Iscariot

Jesus Had Problems With the Twelve:

1. _____ (Matthew 16:9; Mark 4:13; 8:21; Luke 9:45; John 12:16;

   John 20:9 and 24:45)

2. _____ (Mark 9:34; Matthew 18:1-4; Luke 9:46-48)

3. _____ (Matthew 8:26; 14:31; 16:8)

4. _____ (Luke 22:31; John 17:15)

Application

This lesson is full of many amazing teachings and miracles of Christ as well as His calling of the apostles. Discuss the following thoughts and questions with your class based on what you have just studied:

• Share one insight that jumped out to you after reading the Sermon on the Mount in Matthew chapter 5.

• Jesus gives us a beautiful model of prayer in what we call the "Lord's Prayer." Each line of this 52-word prayer can teach us how to pray. For example, "Give us this day our daily bread," can teach us to ask for strength for each day—taking one day at a time. Which part of the prayer most impacts you? Take a moment to pray (individually) that the Lord would continue to teach you in this area of prayer.

Redeemer
Rejected

During this period Jesus was rejected by nearly everyone.

To prepare for class: Read Luke 9:51-62; Matthew 11-12; John 7-10

Write your thoughts and reflections from the reading:

Jesus Christ is Rejected

We will study three events during this period:

1.

2.

3.

By Friends and Family
(Mark 6:1-6)

Jesus was rejected in his home town.

He could do no miracles in Nazareth. Why? What does this mean?

Mark 6:5 He could not do any miracles there, except lay his hands on a few sick people and heal them.

By the "Faithful"

The Pharisees hated Him because (Matthew 15:1-14) …

The Sadducees hated Him because (Matthew 22:23) …

The Samaritans did not welcome Him because (Luke 9:51-56) …

By His Followers
(John 6:53-71)

1. These disciples couldn't accept certain teaching.

2. Jesus had spoken to them _____ and _____.

3. _____ disciples turned back and _____ _____ followed.

4. The words of Simon Peter… "_____."

Application

This lesson deals with the period of rejection in Christ's ministry when many hated Him and some of His own followers even turned away. Discuss the following thoughts and questions with your class based on this difficult period in Christ's ministry:

- The Pharisees were legalistic and did not like Jesus because He did not fit into their system of law. The Sadducees did not believe in Jesus' teachings about a resurrection and they also thought Jesus did not fit into their system of politics.

- The Samaritans did not accept Jesus because he was on His way to Jerusalem and therefore a friend of their enemy. Which of these groups of people are you most like in your acceptance or rejection of Jesus? If you feel comfortable, share you thoughts with the class.

Redeemer   **Lesson 9**
NowHere

In this period Jesus serves notice that He is the Christ!

To prepare for class: Read Luke 9-12

Write your thoughts and reflections from the reading:

Jesus Christ is NowHere

We will study three events during this period:

1.

2.

3.

Here He Is – Testimony
(Matthew 16:13-20)

Some thought that Jesus was a _____ _____.

Simon Peter believed that Jesus was _____ _____.

This passage is one of the few passages where Jesus mentions the _____.

"On this rock…" What is the rock?

The _____ of Hades shall not _____.

This means we are to be the ___ _____!

The _____ to the kingdom were given to Peter.

What does this mean?

Jesus warned them not to share that He is the _____.

Here He Is – Transfiguration
(Luke 9:28-36)

They went up into a mountain.

Jesus' appearance changed. How?

God is _____ .

Moses and Elijah — What do they signify?

- ·

- ·

- ·

The conversation on the mountain —

Here He Is – Telling
(Luke 10:1-24)

The purpose of this mission —

The instructions for the mission —

The cities condemned —

The results of this mission—

Jesus' Response to the Seventy-two

1. I saw Satan _____.

2. You are _____.

3. Do not rejoice over…

4. Your eyes and ears…

Application

The period of "NowHere," studied in this lesson, is an exciting period of Christ's ministry as He notifies the world that He is the Messiah. Discuss the following thoughts and questions with your class based on the three events Christ used during this period to announce and confirm who He is:

- Matthew 16:18 states, "And I tell you that you are Peter, and on this rock I will build my church, and the gates of Hades will not overcome it." As discussed in this lesson, we, as Christians, are to be the aggressors with what we believe. We are to live as victorious and confident people in our faith in Jesus Christ. We are not to fear Satan, but realize that Jesus Himself says the gates of Hades will not overcome His Church! We are His Church! Spend some time in prayer individually. First, confess your sins and your fears. Then, pray for God's power and courage in your own life and specifically that He would give you courage to live out your faith without fear. Finally, pray for your local church body.

Redeemer

Lesson 10

Abhorred/Adored

During this period Jesus is truly hated by his enemies and while they seek a way to destroy Him, it seems that He intentionally makes them more angry.

To prepare for class: Read Luke 13:1 - 19:27

Write your thoughts and reflections from the reading:

Jesus Christ is Abhorred/Adored

We will study three events during this period:

1.

2.

3.

The period begins —

Luke 9:51   As the time approached for him to be taken up to heaven, Jesus resolutely set out for Jerusalem.

Arise, Lazarus
(John 11)

Jesus did not hurry.

The disciples' fear and lack of understanding —

The response of Thomas —

Lazarus had been dead for four days!

What is the significance of this?

Mary and Martha —

This miracle is a _____ and not a _____!

But it is the _____ miracle of Jesus' ministry.

The response to this miracle (John 11:45-53) —

1.

2.

3.

Angers Church Leaders
(Luke 13-19)

As if the raising of Lazarus wasn't enough, Jesus began some of His most difficult teaching. This teaching angered church leaders!

Only a few will be saved (Luke 13)

Teaching in a Pharisee's home — the Sabbath (Luke 14)

The parable of the great banquet (Luke 14)

The parable of the lost sheep/coin (Luke 15)

The parable of the prodigal son (Luke 15)

The rich man and Lazarus (Luke 16)

The kingdom of heaven (Luke 17)

The parable of Pharisee and tax collector (Luke 18)

The parable of the ten minas (Luke 19)

What Was Jesus Doing With This Teaching?

What is the Thrust of This Teaching?

Anointed by Mary
(John 12:1-8)

The purpose of the dinner —

The sacrifice of Mary —

Judas Iscariot —

The purpose of the anointing —

The irony of the chief priest's plans —

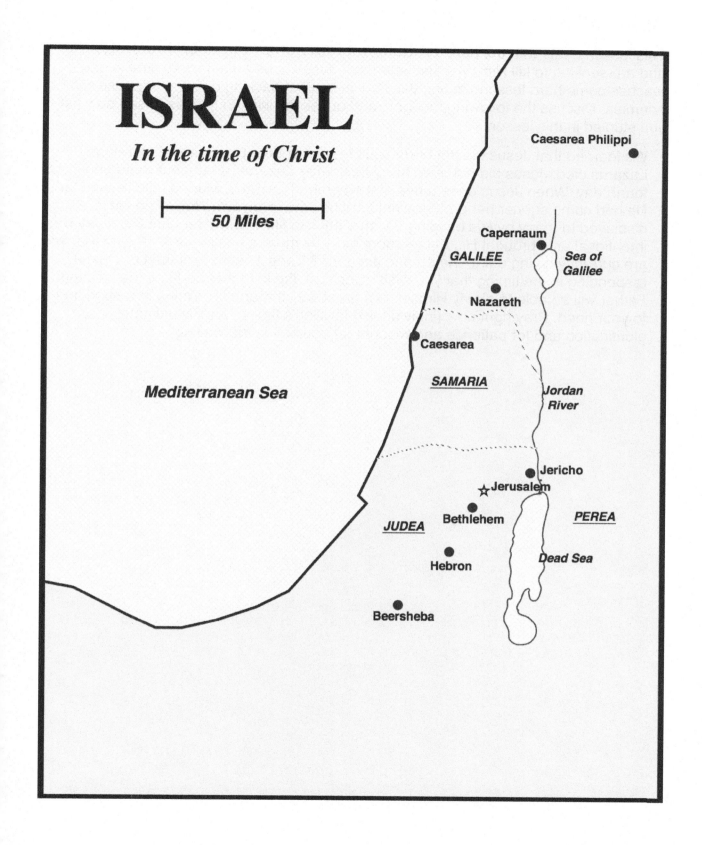

Application

This lesson deals with the period in Christ's ministry where His enemies truly hate Him and are seeking to kill Him. We also learn that Jesus does an amazing miracle and teaches some hard lessons during this time instead of backing down to appease His enemies. Discuss the following thoughts and questions with your class based on what you studied in this lesson:

- We learned that Jesus did not hurry back to heal or help Lazarus and therefore Lazarus died. Jesus did not even hurry back after Lazarus' death, but waited until the fourth day. When Jesus does arrive at the home of Lazarus, Martha tells Jesus that if He had come sooner her brother would still be alive. However, Jesus' power is displayed to many by His bringing Lazarus back to life and we see that His delay was intentional as it brought His Father more glory. Is there a healing or a request that you are currently crying out to the Lord to act upon? Does it seem as if the Lord is not responding in the timing that you wish? Consider the idea that perhaps the Heavenly Father will be able to glorify Himself in a great way through His timing in responding to your need. Pray right now (individually) for God's timing, for His ultimate glorification and for patience and wisdom for yourself in the waiting.

Redeemer

The Passion - Part 1

Lesson 11

This period of Christ's life involves only one week but it is the focus of all Christianity. This week has come to be known as "The Passion."

To prepare for class: Read Luke 19:1 - 22:71

Write your thoughts and reflections from the reading:

Jesus Christ and The Passion

We will study five events during this period:

1. The Triumphal Entry shows Christ as _____.

2. The Temple Cleansing shows Christ as _____.

3. The Tough Teaching shows Christ as _____.

4. The Last Supper shows Christ as _____.

5. The Crucifixion shows Christ as _____.

This seven-day period is the apex of Jesus' ministry and the nucleus of Christianity.

Triumphal Entry
(Luke 19:28-44)

Jesus was serving notice of His _____.

The people wanted a _____ kingdom.

Jesus said that His kingdom was _____ _____. (Luke 17:21)

The people cried "Hosanna" which means...

Jesus will fulfill His earthly kingship...

Temple Cleansing
(Luke 19:45, 46)

This instance is the second time that Jesus drove away the money-changers.

By this act, Jesus was showing His _____.

"House of Prayer" and "Den of Thieves" —

The "authorities" couldn't retaliate because...

Toughest Teaching

These were Jesus' sharpest and most painful parables!

Cursing the fig tree (Matt. 21:18-20)

The parable of the two sons (Matt. 21:28-32)

The parable of the wicked tenants (Luke 20:9-16)

Woes against the Pharisees (Matt. 23)

Prophecies of doom (Luke 21:5-19)

Prophecies on the end of the age (Matt. 24)

The parable of the ten virgins (Matt. 25:1-13)

The parable of the talents (Matt. 25:14-30)

The parable of the true vine (John 15:1-11)

What Do We See in This Teaching?

The Last Supper
(Luke 22:7-23)

1. Jesus celebrated the _____ with His disciples.

   This is not just a meal:

2. He taught them about _____.

3. He names the _____.

4. He institutes _____ _____.

5. He goes to the garden to _____.

6. Judas _____ and later Peter _____.

Application

This lesson deals with the last week of Christ's life here on earth, called The Passion. We learned in this lesson about the Triumphal Entry, the Temple Cleansing, Jesus' Toughest Teachings and the Last Supper. Discuss the following thoughts and questions with your group based on these events that occurred in the last week of Jesus' life:

- Look back in the lesson to the list of parables and teachings along with their respective Scripture references (this is under the heading of Toughest Teaching). Of this list, which of these teachings most impacts you and why? If you feel comfortable, share your thoughts with the class.

- After the Last Supper, Jesus goes to the Garden of Gethsemane. It is late in the evening and he has just had a full meal. On top of this, He knows that the hour is drawing very near to when He will be arrested (unjustly!) and killed. In the midst of these circumstances, we see Jesus praying. We see that Jesus did not desire to suffer but asked the Father to "take the cup" from Him. However, Jesus also prayed not for His own will, but for His Father's will—even in the face of a terrible death. Jesus models for us the importance of praying in all circumstances as well as praying for the Father's will. We see that it is not wrong to tell the Father our desires, but we must seek His will above our own. Is there something you desire in your life right now? Have you prayed specifically to the Father about it? Have you prayed for His will in the situation? Pray now about these things.

Redeemer

The Passion - Part 2

This period of Christ's life involves only one week but it is the focus of all Christianity. This week has come to be known as "The Passion."

To prepare for class: Read Luke 23

Write your thoughts and reflections from the reading:

Jesus Christ and The Passion

We will study five events during this period:

1.

2.

3.

4.

5.

The Crucifixion
(John 18:1 - 19:30)

The Arrest

The "garden" (Gethsemane) —

The request —

The cup —

The kiss —

John's gospel —

The Trial

Jewish leaders (a religious trial) —

To Pilate —

To Herod —

Back to Pilate —

The result —

A Wednesday or Friday Crucifixion?

The traditional Friday Crucifixion —

Sun.	Mon.	Tues.	Wed.	Thurs.	Fri.	Sat.	Sun.

The possible Wednesday Crucifixion —

Sun.	Mon.	Tues.	Wed.	Thurs.	Fri.	Sat.	Sun.

6 o'clock in the evening

Mon.	Tues.	Wed.	Thurs.	Fri.	Sat.	Sun.	

Possible rationale for a Wednesday Crucifixion —

1. three _____ and three _____ (Matt. 12:40; 1 Cor. 15:3-4)

2. the feast days of Leviticus 23

3. the _____ Sabbaths of Matthew 28

4. the _____ Sabbath of John 19:31

5. the _____ hours in a day (John 11:19)

The Trials Before the Authorities

A Roman Crucifixion

The Seven "Words" on the Cross

Luke 23:34	1.
Luke 23:43	2.
John 19:26-27	3.
Matt. 27:46	4.
John 19:28	5.
John 19:30	6.
Luke 23:46	7.

Three Times Jesus Said "It is finished!":

1. John 17:4 —

2. John 19:30 —

3. Rev. 21:6 —

How Do We Know That He Was Really Dead?

1.

2.

3.

4.

5.

6.

7.

Application

In this lesson we study the death of Jesus Christ commonly called "The Crucifixion." Discuss the following thoughts and questions with your class based on the events leading up to Christ's death:

• Jesus told His disciples at the Last Supper that He would be establishing a new covenant "in my blood, which is poured out for you." This new covenant is vital to us: when Jesus died and poured out His blood at the Crucifixion He conquered sin and death and made a way to redeem us and bring us into a relationship with the Heavenly Father. No longer are we under the Law of the Old Testament or have to sacrifice animals to cover our sins as Jesus' sacrifice now pays for all our sin if we are willing to accept Him. Do you understand this new covenant? Have you made a personal decision to accept Christ's sacrifice (for you!) and to have a personal relationship with the God of this universe? If not, and you would like to do so, please talk to your leader after class. If so, hopefully studying again the sacrifice and death of Jesus causes you to be grateful and drawn to worship. Take some time to thank and worship the Lord right now!

---

thē-ŏl'ə-jē

Justification — It is the judicial act of God, by which he pardons all the sins of those who believe in Christ, and accounts, accepts, and treats them as righteous in the eye of the law.

Bryant, T.A. Today's Dictionary of the Bible. Minneapolis, MN: Bethany House Publishers: 1982.

Redeemer   Lesson 13
Exalted

The last period of Christ's earthly ministry is called "Exalted." God the Father exalted His son Jesus because His work was finished! There are three events in the period of Exalted: Empty Tomb (or Easter), Eleven Appearances and Elevated. This period lasted forty days.

To prepare for class: Read Luke 24

Write your thoughts and reflections from the reading:

Jesus Christ is Exalted

We will study three events during this period:

1.

2.

3.

This forty-day period is the last of Jesus' time on earth.

Empty Tomb (Easter)
(John 20:1-17)

Easter Sunday is the _____ of Christianity.

Jesus defeated _____ at the cross but He defeated _____ on Easter.

Sin and death are the two great enemies of man.

The women went to the tomb early to _____ the body.

___ _____ appeared to the women.

Peter and John ran to the tomb, _____ believing.

Jesus appeared _____ to Mary of Magdala.

This is the first time that Jesus ever called the disciples _____! (John 20:17)

Did Jesus Really Come Out of the Tomb

What evidence do we have?

1.

2.

3.

4.

5.

What Theories Are There to Suggest That Jesus Did Not Rise From the Dead?

1. _____ Theory.

   Response?

2. The disciples _____. (Matt. 28:11-15)

   Response?

3. The disciples _____.

   Response?

4. The Romans or Jews _____.

   Response?

5. The women and disciples _____.

   Response?

6. Others?

Eleven Appearances

Jesus appeared at least eleven times to followers after the resurrection:

1. to the women (Matt. 28:9-10)

2. to Mary alone (John 20:14)

3. to Peter alone (Luke 24:34)

4. to the disciples on Emmaus Road (Luke 24:13-35)

5. to ten apostles in Jerusalem (John 20:19)

6. to the eleven apostles (John 20:26-29)

7. to seven disciples in Galilee (John 21:1-14)

8. to all the apostles on a mountain (Matt. 28:18-20)

9. to five hundred brethren all at once (1 Cor. 15:6)

10. to James alone (1 Cor. 15:7)

11. to the group on the Mount of Ascension (Luke 24:51)

What Do We Learn From These Appearances?

God's Feast Days and Their Relationship to Christ

Feast	Length	When Held	Don't	Do	Reason for Feast	Fulfillment
Sabbath	1 day	Every seventh day	Work	Assemble	A time to rest and celebrate the Lord and His creation	
Passover and Unleavened Bread	7 days	14th and 15th day of First month (Nisan)	Work on first and seventh day	Assemble, eat bread made without yeast	A time to remember the exodus from Egypt	
First Fruits	1 day	Day following the Sabbath after Passover	Eat any grain	Sacrifice Lamb	The first fruits of the field are showing	
Feast of Weeks	1 day	Fifty days after First Fruits	Work	Assemble, make offering	Harvest is now complete; be thankful	
Feast of Trumpets	1 day	First day of the seventh month (Tishri)	Work	Assemble, blow trumpets, make offering	The new year; celebrate and be thankful	
Day of Atonement	1 day	Tenth day of seventh month	Work	Assemble, and fast	The day of judging man's sin	
Feast of Tabernacles	7 days	Fifteenth day of seventh month	Work on first and seventh day	Assemble, make offering	Remember God dwelling with His people	

What Do We Learn From the Feast Days?

1.

2.

3.

4.

5.

Elevated — Ascension
(Luke 24:50-52 and Acts 1:9-11)

What was the purpose of the ascension?

1.

2.

3.

4.

5.

Application

This lesson covers the centerpiece of Christianity, the resurrection of Jesus Christ from the dead. Discuss the following thoughts and questions with your class based on this wonderful miracle:

- If Jesus Christ rose from the dead then there is no reason to ever reject Him as God. He is truly Who He says He is. Do you believe this miracle really happened? As a testimony to God's great power in conquering both sin and death by rising from the dead, share with your class what evidence leads you to believe in Jesus' resurrection and also share what impact this has had on your life.

New Testament Theological Terms and Definitions

Redemption

The purchase back of something that had been lost, by the payment of a ransom. (Lesson 1)

Incarnation

That act of grace whereby Christ took our human nature into union with his divine person—became man. (Lesson 4)

Justification

It is the judicial act of God, by which He pardons all the sins of those who believe in Christ, and accounts, accepts, and treats them as righteous in the eye of the law. (Lesson 12)

Prayer List

Request	Date	Answer	Date

Prayer List

Request	Date	Answer	Date

Prayer List

Request	Date	Answer	Date

Prayer List

Request	Date	Answer	Date

Prayer List

Request	Date	Answer	Date

Prayer List

Request	Date	Answer	Date

Prayer List

Request	Date	Answer	Date

Prayer List

Request	Date	Answer	Date

Prayer List

Request	Date	Answer	Date

Prayer List

Request	Date	Answer	Date

Prayer List

Request	Date	Answer	Date

Prayer List

Request	Date	Answer	Date

Prayer List

Request	Date	Answer	Date

Prayer List

Request	Date	Answer	Date

Prayer List

Request	Date	Answer	Date

Prayer List

Request	Date	Answer	Date

Prayer List

Request	Date	Answer	Date

Notes

Notes

Notes

Notes

Notes

Notes

Notes

Notes

Notes

Notes